# Inclusive Capitalism
## What It Looks Like In Practice

The Story of How the PSN Corporation Became the Growth Leader in the Industrial Fastener Industry

By

Leonard C. Scott
Dallas, Texas

Copyright 2013

About the Author

Leonard C. Scott is a human resources professional with more than forty years in the field. He has been a corporate human resources and labor relations executive, has provided human resources consulting services to a broad range of American and foreign owned companies, and has taught business and human resources management course at several colleges. He has appeared on a number of radio talk shows and made presentations at national and international professional and trade associations. His educational background includes undergraduate and graduate credentials from the University of Illinois, Northwestern University, and Cornell University. He lives in Dallas and can be reached at scottco@airmail.net His website is found at www. lenscottandcompany.com It contains information on his books, articles, programs, and presentations.

# Contents

| | |
|---|---|
| Introduction | 3 |
| Chapter I — Inclusive Capitalism at the PSN Corporation | 5 |
| Attachment 1 — Progressive Wage Payment Plan | 12 |
| Attachment 2 — How To Build a Turbo-Charged Sales Force | 27 |
| Attachment 3 —Establishing an Effective Human Resources Program | 48 |
| Chapter II — How Inclusive Capitalism Will Solve Many of the Country's Economic Problems | 57 |
| Chapter III — The Road to Inclusive Capitalism, a New Set of Labor Laws and a New Business School Curriculum | 63 |

Introduction

Inclusive Capitalism is seen as the path to rebuilding the Middle Class and solving the economic growth, unemployment, and underemployment problem. But what is Inclusive Capitalism? Inclusive Capitalism is an economic system wherein the businesses and organizations within it are characterized by progressive policies and practices such as paying a living wage, profit sharing, employee speak out meetings, employee complaint resolution programs, in-house training programs to fill job openings, employee training and development programs to enable employees to reach the highest level of their ability, performance appraisal systems, innovation and creativity bonuses for rank and file employees as well as managerial and executive employees, full blown employee motivation programs*, and work rules that allow for continuity of employment.

This book tells the story of an Inclusive Capitalism company, the PSN Corporation, that became the growth leader in the industrial fastener industry in the 1970s by virtue of its Inclusive Capitalism

---

* See Leonard C. Scott's <u>A Quick Guide To Employee Motivation, Thirty-Three Proven Employee Motivation Concepts To Make Your Company A Winner</u>.

approach to operating its business. The story is told through the eyes of the Human Resources Director who is the author of this book.

Chapter I — Inclusive Capitalism at the PSN Corporation

I was hired by the PSN Company, a manufacturer of industrial fasteners (screws, nuts, and bolts), in Elk Grove, Illinois, a suburb of Chicago, because it was having serious difficulties securing workers to operate its production equipment. With the Viet Nam War drawing more and more young men into service, the labor market was very tight. However, I found early on that in addition to hiring an adequate work force, one of the two brothers who owned the company wanted to build a business that was very profitable, growth oriented, innovative in style, and most importantly, fun to operate, yes, fun to operate. He believed that if a company secured the best people, paid them well, had them work in teams, provided them with the very best equipment and work environment, regularly communicated with them, trained them fully to do their jobs, and shared financial gains with them, the company would be a resounding success. The story that follows is how PSN grew from a "ma and pa" shop status to industry growth leader and the role I played in this wonderful success story.

The first task I was given was to hire people for the factory. It was experiencing a 30% monthly turnover, and 25% of the machines were unmanned. Before I could start hiring plant people, I had to determine what they should be paid in order to attract the right people in the right number. To do that I used a standard industrial type job evaluation system to rank the plant jobs. A wage curve about 6% above the going rates, which I secured from the U.S. Department of Labor Chicago Area Wage Surveys, was overlain on this structure. This determined where the starting and base wage rates should be set. Starting rates were about 6% above those paid in the area at the time. The key element in the wage payment plan was the method by which employees moved from starting rate to base rate and beyond if outstanding performance justified that. The payment plan (See Attachment 1) was a progressive one; that is, it started out with an above market starting rate, provided interim rates as the worker became more proficient at and productive in his/her job, and then offered a base rate to the employee who was fully qualified in his/her working and performing at the accepted level of output. A merit wage range was made available to those few more senior employees who consistently performed above the accepted standard. The wage progression was tied directly to the experience factor in the job evaluation system. For example, jobs that were evaluated as having an 18 month learning curve, had 18 month wage progressions. Those with a 12 month learning curve had 12 month wage progressions, and so forth. The rates proceeded to increase from starting rate to the next higher rate after one month and then at three-month intervals until the basic wage rate was reached. The increases were usually granted in accord with the wage payment progression, except where a department manager wished to hold up an increase for a period of time or grant a quick increase or double jump increase after a three month period of time. This wage payment plan had the characteristic of motivating employees significantly. The department manager had full authority to delay an increase or initiate quick or double jump increases with the Human Resources Director reviewing them for adherence to the wage schedule and the Plant Manager having the final decision with respect to delaying or granting the increase. Employees liked the wage payment plan because they had the opportunity to get an increase every three months up until they reached the basic wage rate in their classifications. The department managers like it because it motivated their employees, but still enabled them to hold up increases for slow learners or problem employees. They also had the ability to grant quick increases or double jump increases for the fast track employees, the highly motivated, efficient workers in their departments. The Personnel Director liked the system because it enabled him to recruit above average workers in a tight labor market. The accounting department liked the system because they could budget labor costs accurately in that they knew what increases would be granted and when they would be granted. The Plant Manager liked the system because he could maintain overall control of wage costs in the plant. Another characteristic of this wage payment plan was a range of wages above the area surveyed base rates for the various jobs. This range, which amounted to about a 7% spread, was called the merit rate range, and the rates in it could be given to employees with significant seniority and consistent above standard output. This was a very attractive plum which department managers could offer senior superstars in their departments. This merit range was regarded by the employees as a very fair way to compensate people who had been with the company for some time and who expended extra effort or were particularly skilled in their work. The use of this progressive wage payment plan enabled me to completely staff the plant, cut down on turnover, and to speed up the learning curve in the various classifications. It really solved the plant turnover problem.

The next major task that the company undertook was the securing of qualified trainees to learn various set-up man and operator jobs. There was a large shortage of young men due to the Viet Nam conflict. The manufacture of fasteners is a very noisy, dusty, dirty operation and it has difficulty attracting people in the best of times. To react to this situation, I convinced the owners that the company should establish an in-house set-up man training program. The president ordered the plant manager to remove several older cold heading machines from the production lines, place them in a separate training area, chose a very skilled set-up man with excellent training skills to act as the program trainer, and provided him with all the tools, equipment, space, and training materials that he needed to get the job done. He needed to train "green hands" with the requisite qualifications to become cold header set-up men. This was a very expensive proposition, but in terms of the results, a very profitable one over the long run. Over a period of three years some 60% of the set-up men in the company were brought into their jobs through the in-house training program. It enabled the company to stop competing with other firms for the small number of experienced set-up men who were jumping from one company to another for 25 cent or 50 cent wage increases and build its own well qualified set-up man force which was loyal, stable, and without the bad habits that many of the experienced set-up man had picked up over the years. The new set-up man trainees were screened through the use of a mechanical comprehension test, the Wonderlic Test (a test of basic problem solving ability), personal interviews, and background and reference checks. Those who showed that they had the mechanical and mental aptitude and acceptable employment track record to succeed in the training program were hired. Even with the use of these screening devices, the turnover in the training program was 50%. As a result of the plant wage payment plan, the set-up man training program, and the delegation to the department managers of virtually complete responsibility for running their departments, the plant began to function in a highly productive manner. The managers had, perhaps for the first time in their working lives, the responsibility for hiring, firing, training, disciplining, and setting wage rates of their employees. They were also responsible for output, quality, administration, and housekeeping which they delegated to each individual employee. The department managers truly ran their departments in their entirety. The Plant Manager worked with these managers and solved with them many technical and production issues, but he never micro-managed them. They were on their own to succeed or fail. This freedom to operate their areas of responsibility motivated them immensely. They began to move faster, think faster, ask more questions, display new found self confidence, and be much more decisive. Along with this new responsibility, the department managers were given a good dose of management training. This educational program exposed them to motivation techniques, leadership approaches, discipline and discharge methods, counseling techniques, budgeting, and establishing statistics for determining department performance.

Attachment 1 — WAGE PAYMENT PLAN — PLANT

A. POLICY
1. Payment Structure

The determination of a starting rate (which shall be a rate in the established wage structure) for any new employee will be the responsibility of the department head who hires the individual. The department head may delegate to the Personnel Director his/her hiring authority with respect to the employment of inexperienced workers. In this case the Personnel Manager would determine the starting rate. The wage payment plan contains four classifications of wage rates:

a. Stating Rate — wage rate used for period of orientation and observation. This rate is paid to a newly hired employee who has no experience in the work of the classification into which he is hired

b. Training Wage Rates — a range of starting rates for partially qualified employees (those who have some experience in the work of the classification into which they are hired.) and a scale of interim wage rates to be used for inexperienced employees as they progress in their training toward the fully qualified level of job performance.

c. Basic Wage Rates — wage rates which are comparable to those paid in the area and industry for similar work for employees who have been recognized by management to be fully capable of performing the requirements of the job.

Merit Wage Rates — wage rates for fully qualified employees with substantial service for consistent above normal effort.

2. Shift Premium
A shift premium of 10% is paid for work in the scheduled second and third shifts.

3. Probationary Period
A three month probationary period will apply to all hourly employees.

## B. WAGE RATE DETERMINATION

1. At time of hire the Human Resources Director and the department head will determine if the worker being employed is completely inexperienced in the work of the job into which he is moving, partially experienced in this work, or fully experienced in these duties. If the employee is completely inexperienced, his/her beginning rate will be the starting rate of the classification. If the employee is partially qualified, his/her beginning rate will be one of the training rates. If the employee is fully qualified, his/her beginning rate will be the 'A' training rate of the Basic Wage Rate minus ten cents. (A rate of the Basic Wage Rate minus ten cents may be granted to a new employee only with the approval of the Plant Manager.) The department head should determine the appropriate beginning rate for partially qualified employees. Should a department head have difficulty in determining the beginning rate of a partially qualified employee, he should consult with the Personnel Director and the Plant Manager.

2. The time interval between performance reviews is as follows:

Starting Rate — First Training Rate = One month (raise may be delayed only on month

One Training Rate to another
Training Rate = Three months (raise may be delayed up to two months)

Training Rate A to Basic Wage Rate and Basic Wage Rate minus ten cents to Basic Wage rate = Three months (raise may be delayed up to two months)

The wage rates shown in the various wage progressions will be granted according to the schedule on a performance basis only.

An inexperienced employee hired at a starting rate will not receive his first performance review until one month has elapsed from date of hire. A department head may give him a raise immediately after his first month of employment or delay it up to another month. No further delays in this case will be approved for sub-standard performance. He must be discharged if the department head cannot justify giving him a raise after his second month of employment.

A partially qualified employee starting at a given training rate will not receive his first performance review until three (3) months have elapsed from date of hire. This rule also applies to fully qualified employees. If a department head wishes to bring partially qualified employee up to the next rate in the progression or bring a fully qualified employee up to the Basic wage Rate from training rate A or from ten cents below the Basic Wage rate in less than three months, he must put through a wage increase for the employee. A department head may delay a wage increase for one month on his own authority. He may delay a wage increase for an additional one month with approval of the Plant Manager, Director of Manufacturing, and Personnel Manager. Approval for a delay in a wage increase will not be given where the delay period is more than two months.

Employees not performing at the level dictated by their training rate or Basic Wage Rate must be so informed, warned that disciplinary action will be taken if no improvement is made and finally discharged if no improvement is forthcoming. In cases of sub-standard performance, discharge must not be delayed longer than one or two months following date of performance review—three months following prior raises. The steps in all such disciplinary cases must be documented in writing by the department head.

3. One double jump increase, e.g., from Training Rate C to a Training Rate A, and one quick raise, e.g., increase from one training rate to another in less than three months or an

increase from Training Rate A to the Basic Wage Rate in less than three months, may be given an employee while in a given classification. The personnel manager will be responsible for administering this provision of the Wage Payment Plan.

4. Guide lines for Granting Merit Range Raises
A. Employee must be at top rate in classification for at least six months.
B. No merit increase may be greater than twenty cents.
C. Merit increases must be separated from each other by at least six months.
D. No merit increase may bring an employee's wage rate above the maximum merit wage rate for the classification.

5. An employee temporarily assigned to another classification will carry his current rate in his classification unless he is fully qualified in the classification to which he is assigned and once received the Basic Wage rate while in that classification. In that case the employee will be paid the Basic Wage Rate of the classification to which he is temporarily assigned.

## WAGE RATE SHEETS

### Dept. 100 - Toolroom

| Classification Title | Staring Rt | Training Rates | | | | | | BWR | M.MWR |
| --- | --- | --- | --- | --- | --- | --- | --- | --- | --- |
| | | F | E | D | C | B | A | | |
| Die Maker A | 9.94 | 10.10 | 10.26 | 10.43 | 10.67 | 10.93 | 11.09 | 11.23 | 11.53 |
| Die Maker B | 9.83 | | 9.91 | 10.07 | 10.23 | 10.39 | 10.54 | 10.70 | 10.95 |

### Dept. 130 – Maintenance

| Classification Title | Staring Rt. | F | E | D | C | B | A | BWR | M.MWR |
| --- | --- | --- | --- | --- | --- | --- | --- | --- | --- |
| Maint. Man A | 9.94 | 10.10 | 10.26 | 10.43 | 10.67 | 10.93 | 11.09 | 11.23 | 11.53 |
| Maint. Man B | 9.80 | | | 9.89 | 10.03 | 10.19 | 10.31 | 10.42 | 10.66 |
| Janitor | 8.28 | | | | | | | 8.37 | 8.53 |

Dept. 200 – Heading

| Classification Title | Starting Rt. | F | E | D | C | B | A | BWR | MMWR |
|---|---|---|---|---|---|---|---|---|---|
| Set--Up | 9.85 | 9.93 | 10.10 | 10.26 | 10.42 | 10.55 | 10.67 | 10.80 | 11.09 |
| Trucker/Wire | 8.72 | | | | 8.83 | 8.93 | 9.04 | 9.15 | 9.37 |

As I completed the implementation of this new management and wage payment system in manufacturing, I began recruiting various members of the executive team. The targets for these recruiting activities were Fortune 500 companies and the Major Public Accounting firms. The individuals sought were persons with an entrepreneurial orientation, that is, those who were not comfortable within the rigid organizational structure in which they were operating. These new executives were expected to enjoy working in a fast moving, high risk/high reward environment. Some executive search firms were employed in this activity, but the majority of the recruiting was done through carefully worded display employment ads, contacts with local university alumni placement directors, employee referrals, and direct contact of industry individuals whose reputations had come to the attention of the company owners. Executives were hired in the areas of manufacturing, accounting, sales and marketing, and information systems. These individuals and those already in the company were joined in an executive committee, which reported to the two owners through the sales and marketing executive who had been raised to the position of Executive Vice President. The various middle managers reported to the members of this committee. The strategy with respect to the establishment of this committee was the building of close teamwork among the top managers. I chose to use salaried job evaluation and salary administration to begin the process of team building. Once the executive committee was in place the first order of business was the task of evaluating and slotting all the salaried positions in the company. A simple fifteen slot ranking system was chosen with various benchmark jobs inserted as pegs in the system. It was very quick and surprisingly accurate. Also, it enabled the members of the executive committee to interact on a regular basis, hammering out compromises on the slotting of jobs and providing insights to each other with respect to job content, focus, and importance. This committee was an excellent vehicle to disseminate information quickly on the various jobs within the company to the various function heads, many of whom were recent arrivals to the company and the industry. Where there was disagreement as to the ranking of a job, the president would have the final vote as to the slotting of the job in question. The compensation levels for the various salaried jobs were generally those paid for similar jobs in the fastener industry. However, these salary ranges were adjusted up by the inclusion of data from much larger companies which were the targets of the company's recruiting efforts, so the ranges would allow for the hiring of executives from these firms. To add motivational impact to the compensation environment in which the executives worked, the salary ranges for these executives were structured so they had no maximums. Without salary maximums, it was theoretically possible for the various members of the executive committee to be paid as much as the chairman felt they were worth and not be topped out in compensation because of a salary range maximum or control point. The motivational impact of this decision with respect to eliminating salary range maximums was tremendous. Executives working with salary ranges that had no maximums were energized to perform well above and beyond the expected levels of achievement, and when some of them reached salary levels which clearly were beyond what they knew their maximum salary level would have been, they worked even harder and more effectively. Also, this salary administration policy enabled PSN to retain the high performance executives that were being solicited by much larger, more established corporations. Money clearly worked as a highly effective motivator and retention device in this case.

This brings us to the next step in the building of the PSN management system, the management by objectives (MBO) program. This MBO program was simple. It involved one sheet of paper completed every six months. The objectives were agreed upon by each function head and his or her superior, and that is what the function heads strove to achieve for the upcoming six months. It was coordinated by the chairman of the board, who saw to it that all of the objectives were consistent with each other and in agreement with the overall company plan. The MBO system was further strengthened by an announcement from the Chairman that if an executive committee member did not achieve his/her goals over a year period, he/she would be asked to leave the company, but outplacement assistance would be provided so that he/she would maintain his/her income stream until getting another job. In other words, "playing it safe" was taken out of top management's attempts to achieve their objectives. This resulted in incredibly innovative approaches to achieve objectives and rapid increases in company growth and profitability. Innovation in the company poured forth at an unbelievable pace. To compensate for this well above-average outpouring of effort, energy, insight and innovation, a bonus system was established for the management group. This bonus plan was tied to company profitability and individual achievement of objectives. This bonus plan went right down to the department manager level and resulted in all the managers and executives in the company working closely with each other with minimum risk, almost no politics, and no fear of experimentation. As the company developed, I wrote a personnel policy manual. This particular manual was kept flexible. It was reviewed in terms of its effectiveness virtually every month. Those policies that were deemed ineffective or inappropriate were changed. Very little was cast in concrete. It was kept competitive according to industry and area standards, but it provided for openness, flexibility, and experimentation with respect to holidays, vacation pay, open employee speak-out meetings, and other areas related to working conditions.

To enlist the continuing support of the rank and file employees in this rapidly growing, high stress company, an employee speak out program was established. Every year, all employees in groups of five to ten met with the Chairman of the Board to air their grievances, make suggestions for improving operations, and express their satisfactions. These meetings lasted approximately twenty minutes to a half hour and were conducted over a period of about a month. I took notes and followed up on the changes that were suggested and approved and saw to it that they were implemented. Also, I followed up on the suggestions that were not approved and passed back to the employees the reasons the suggestions were not adopted. This communications program brought all the employees into direct contact with the top decision makers in the company. Finally, to enlist the full cooperation of the rank and file employees, a profit sharing plan was established. It was fully explained to the employees, and in general it ran in a very open manner with respect to investments, contributions, and administrative matters.

The executive committee worked hard to establish a corporate culture that was supportive of the rapid growth strategy of the company. The firm was so effective at sales and marketing that it sold 25% more product than it produced. This increment in sales was purchased from other manufacturers and dropped shipped by these firms to PSN's customers. This difference between production and sales was planned and resulted in generating a strong sense of security among everyone in the company. The fear of employment cutbacks as a result of poor economic conditions was greatly decreased.

When all is said and done, PSN's success was seen to result from its sales activity. PSN was a turbo-charged sales machine. Many war stories grew up with respect to the sales department. It was clearly seen as the powerful locomotive that was taking the company up the track to its very lofty growth objectives. It was commonplace to see salesmen go out into the plant to talk to department managers, set-up men, and production employees. This interaction resulted in the salesmen imparting their enthusiasm to the workers in the plant and warehouse, and shipping department.

While all this corporate culture building was going on, the usual nuts and bolts personnel instruments were developed. A company newspaper was published, an employee activity committee was set up to enable employees to participate in local softball, bowling, and golf leagues, a scholarship program covering the children of employees was created, a safety committee was put into place, and a company picnic planning group was established.

Another major plank in the corporate culture was quality. The president let it be known that the motto of the quality activity in the company was that quality could not be inspected into the product, but had to be built into the product. He then went on to announce that no line inspectors would ever be hired by the company. He made it clear that product quality was 100% the responsibility of each and every employee in the plant. He allowed for the hiring of a few raw materials inspectors and finished goods checkers, but maintained that quality would always be the responsibility of the individual plant employees.

To reinforce the growth of the sales organization and its lead role in generating rapid company growth, various innovative recruiting techniques were employed. First, the selection process for PSN salesmen was very stringent. Salesmen had to look good, communicate well, be bright, be interesting persons, and have exceptional sales aptitude. Every salesman had some kind of interest that in some way made him a special individual. One was a pilot. Another collected antique firearms. Another was a scratch golfer. Still another was an expert unicyclist, and so on. All sales rep applicants were tested for sales aptitude and intelligence. Second, I contacted the business schools at the local universities and listed job openings for sales trainees there. I then offered the heads of the marketing departments of these schools tours of PSN to provide them with first hand exposure to the company's entrepreneurial environment, modern office and plant, and cutting edge management systems and procedures. These contacts with the local business schools paid off handsomely in that year after year the sales trainee class contained the cream of the crop of local business school graduates. Third, newly hired sales reps and sales trainees met regularly in their first year in the company with the Chairman, who was a master telemarketer, and the Executive Vice President, a true sales champion. At these informal lunch meetings, the Chairman and Executive Vice President would impart their knowledge of effective selling techniques and also give them a large dose of the tricks of the trade in sales. These meetings motivated the sales reps and also provided an opportunity for the Chairman and the Executive Vice President to evaluate and coach the sales reps in a very personal manner. The details of this sales recruiting and development program are presented in Attachment 2, in my article "How To Build A Turbo-Charged Sales Force." Further, the sales department was structured on an "inside-outside" basis. The outside salesmen were complete sales professionals. They could generate new business, assist customers with their fastener design needs, and close the toughest, most close resistant prospects. They were truly remarkable salesmen. The inside sales reps were super communicators, great telephone salesmen, and adept at maintaining a positive relationship with the customer through the ups and downs of the business relationship. The outside sales rep and the inside sales rep worked very closely. Their compensation plans were such that they shared commission on the various sales that each made. The motto of the this "outside-inside" sales team was "Even When I'm out, I'm In." Customers took to this motto and always remembered it.

PSN was one of the first computerized firms in the fastener industry. The computer system was used for accounting, inventory control, planning, and budgeting purposes. Also, it was used for a long tine as one of the centerpieces of the company's advertising program. When competitors were showing screws, bots, and cold heading machines in their ads, PSN was showing its computers, shinny faced employees, and its ultra modern office and plant. The company's advertising clearly sent the message that doing business with PSN was doing business with a bright, young, innovative company, clearly on the move. The computer system was regularly updated, and its use as a management tool was constantly expanded.

Attachment 2 —How To Build A Turbo-Charged Sales Force

A turbo-charged sales force—just what is that? Well, it is a sales force which consistently achieves or exceeds its objectives for sales, margin, product mix, customer service, win back, and any other established sales related metric. Building a turbo-charged sales force is a job for the CEO or COO. If it is not undertaken at the top, it just won't happen. A CEO or COO starts building a turbo-charged sales force by understanding and embracing the business philosophy of George Steinbrenner, the now deceased owner of the New York Yankees. It goes like this: "I'm obsessed with winning, with discipline, with achieving." And what goes along with this obsession with winning is the commitment to expend the time and money to put together a sales force head and shoulders above that of any other competitor. Steinbrenner is a model in this area also. His New York Yankees had the highest payroll in baseball. Steinbrenner equated having great players with winning and winning with filling his stadium every day, which gave him an optimum return on investment.

That is it! The basic philosophical foundation for building a turbo-charged sales team then consists of an obsession with winning, a commitment to expend the time and money to secure and train the most effective sales professionals available, and taking the time to interact with and motivate them to the highest level of performance. All the rest deals with technical matters of recruitment, assessment, and transfer of knowledge and proven sales techniques from sales management to senior sales reps, senior sales reps to middle experienced sales reps, and middle experienced sales reps to beginner sales reps and trainees.

The starting point in the technical aspect of building a turbo-charged sales force then is assessment. The use of a test instrument like the Caliper Sales Aptitude Test will get that done. Very likely the results of such a test will be eye opening and explain why the 80/20 rule consistently explains sales force performance at the typical company.

At one of my clients in the building products industry, the assessment of the sales force indicated, as usually is the case, that there was a very close correlation between sales performance and sales aptitude. In that firm, two of the "bottom" performing sales reps showed no sign of having any sales aptitude at all. Their ego drive, or desire to persuade and close, was low; their empathy, or ability to connect with prospects and customers, was low; and their ego strength, ability to bounce back after rejection, was low. I asked the Sales Manager why he hired them and kept them, in light of their lack of sales aptitude and poor sales records. His response: The father of one of these sales reps was one of the company's bigger distributors, and he wanted to get his son into sales. What the Sales Manager was saying was that he was concerned that he might lose this distributor's business if he let this distributor's son go. In the case of the other poor performing sales rep, the Sales Manager said that he really liked the guy and that he worked 60 or 70 hours a week. I reminded the Sales Manager that this rep really wasn't selling much. He agreed and eventually let this sales rep go. However, he kept the other non-performing sales rep because of his fear of losing his father's business. Needless to say, this company never built a turbo-charged sales force. It did satisfactorily in its industry, but never became a leader.

After sales aptitude assessment, the next step is sales training for the sales reps who show strong sales aptitude but perhaps do not have a sufficient grasp of the sales techniques and discipline required to excel. The sales training step provides the opportunity to increase the sales force's selling skills and announce a "two or three strikes and your out" policy, that is, missing sales quotas for two or three quarters in a row will result in employment termination.

While all this is going on, a continuing recruitment program is put into motion which is aimed at doing two things: bringing high level sales performers into the sales team from competitors and near competitors and bringing in young, green talent and trainees with high potential into the "beginner" level of the sales team.

Now, how this is done is critical to getting the right people! The use of an outside recruiter in this effort is all important. The first thing to do because it is more cost effective is contract with an hourly fee recruiter, as opposed to an employment agency or executive search firm, to work with your Sales Manager or Human Resources Manager to conduct this continuing sales rep recruiting program. Where do you find one of these hourly fee recruiters? Look in the Executive Search Research Directory published by Kenneth Cole. Once you contract with an hourly fee recruiter—and make sure you get a six-month or one year replacement guarantee. The first thing to tell him/her to do is keep an eye out for a sales champion. Granted, these super sales manger/performers become available rarely. However, keeping a line out for them is always strategically important. Next, have this recruiter get with your Sales Manager and senior sales reps to identify the top sales reps at competitors and near competitors. These sales professionals sell against these individuals every day and know who they are. Then, have your hourly fee recruiter contact these targets to learn if they have an interest in talking about opportunities at your firm. Of course, the hourly fee recruiter does not identify your firm and maintains strict confidentiality in all aspects of the recruiting contact. Now, you probably are wondering why a top sales rep at a competitor or near competitor would leave an established job and join your firm. Well, the answers are money, benefits, options, and perks, opportunity to work with more high powered sales professionals at a more prestigious firm, chance to sell a better product with better customer service and sales support, and an avenue to get away from an unacceptable boss. Top sales professionals at competitors can be recruited. I have seen this done regularly over the years.

Next have your hourly fee recruiter conduct research on the availability of top sales professionals. Have him/her screen the Internet employment sites and contact the top sales reps at firms with leading sales forces that are downsizing. State WARN reports provide information on firms downsizing and going out of business. These reports provide contact persons, addresses, and phone numbers. Often these downsizing firms are very interested in seeing that their top performers find attractive new positions.

Next, have your Sales Manager and hourly/fee recruiter contact local business school marketing professors to identify and refer their top students interested un getting into sales. These academics know who the winners are in their classes. Contact these students and pass them through your sales trainee evaluation process. Establishing relationships with these professors is not difficult. Make your company available to them for tours; set up internships for their top students; and offer them the opportunity to use your firm for research and special studies.

One of the most over looked locations of individuals who have the potential to become top performing sales reps are non-sale departments in house. The Caliper sales aptitude assessment organization has found that 20% of the population in general have superior sales aptitude than 50% of the individuals who are working as sales reps. That means that in any given company there are likely to be a number of employees in non-sales jobs who have the ability to become high performance sales reps. How do you find out who these employees are? Use the performance appraisal process. Just ask managers which employees they think have strong, but unidentified sales aptitude and then ask these employees if they would like to apply for a sales rep job and enter the sales rep assessment process.

These efforts should provide a steady flow of very high quality sales rep applicants and begin the process of building a turbo-charged sales force.

The next order of business in building a turbo-charged sales force is setting up a program whereby the CEO or COO interacts with and motivates all sales reps in the company on a regular basis. The top company executive who shoulders this responsibility should be prepared to spend an increasing amount of time on sales and sales related matters. He/she should block out time each month to interact with members of the sales force to build pride in employment and esprit'de corps among them. At these meetings, which might be breakfasts, lunches, or dinners, he/she along with the Sales Manager The next order of business in building a turbo-charged sales force is setting up a program whereby the CEO or COO interacts with and motivates all sales reps in the company on a regular basis. The top company executive who shoulders this responsibility should be prepared to spend an increasing amount of time on sales and sales related matters. He/she should block out time each month to interact with members of the sales force to build pride in employment and esprit'de corps among them. At these meetings, which might be breakfasts, lunches, or dinners, he/she along with the Sales Manager should pass on sales "tricks of the trade," new effective selling approaches, information on industry and competitor peculiarities, company culture, and product or service features, benefits, and unique characteristics, and any other information that would be helpful to the sales team. These meetings can build a personal relationship between the top executive and his/her sales team that results in the sales force going above and beyond the call of duty to "make the numbers." At these meetings, the top company executive and the Sales Manager should elicit from the sales team intelligence on what is going on in the market, what competitors are up to, and who the top sales reps at competitors and near competitors are. Also, they should identify the high potential sales reps and flag them for development and promotion. During the glory days of GE in the 1990's, Jack Welsh, GE's CEO, spent 60% of his time interacting with his people. Also, Joe Gibbs, the SuperBowl winning coach of the Washington Redskins and CEO of the NASCAR team that captured the Winston Cup in 2000 and 2002 uses and recommends this people focused management philosophy. He says "I tell any company that I talk to, make sure you spend the most time and money picking employees...and trying to build the best team." This approach does work.

Also, the top company executive in charge of the turbo-charged sales force effort should make it a point to showcase sales reps in company advertising, have sales reps become active in company affairs and community relations activities, and insure that the sales department budget is sufficient to attract, train, and motivate the high quality and high potential sales reps that will take the company to a leadership position.

In building a turbo-charged sales force, the sales rep assessment process should include multiple interviews, extensive reference and background checks, sales aptitude testing, intelligence testing, and role plays. The objective of this process is to build a sales team that has better sales aptitude and sales track record, higher intelligence, better appearance, higher energy, more notable personal interests, and greater initiative and ingenuity than the sales team at any competitor.

Another trick of building a turbo-charged sales force involves counter-cyclical hiring. When are the best sales professionals more likely to be available? The answer: in the down phase of a business or industry cycle when everyone else is letting go sales professionals of all achievement levels. Selective hiring during down times can result in securing sales professionals with exceptional track records and ability. Also, this is the time to cast a net for a sales champion. One of these extremely rare individuals sometimes become available when his/her industry hits a period of serious readjustment. I saw this happen a few years ago when the computer chip industry retrenched drastically.

An effective approach to hiring outstanding low and mid-level experienced sales reps in the building of a turbo-charged sales force is the use of direct response employment ads. These are ads which are placed in the Sunday newspapers Employment Section and on Internet job sites with a standout heading, potential yearly compensation figures, details of the job content, and a phone number to call on Sunday evening or Monday morning to get further details and apply for the position. The contract recruiter or Human Resources Director should take the responses, screen the applicants, and establish a slate for further evaluation later in the week. These ads allow for the creation of a slate of applicants quickly, draw out good prospects who are action oriented and who would otherwise not respond to regular recruitment advertising, and are highly cost effective. These ads interest low and mid-level experienced sales reps who are trolling employment ads to see what is happening in the sales rep labor market and which firms are offering superior compensation packages. The opportunity to respond to these ads immediately, get details on the job and a feel for the company, and set up a quick interview appeals to sales reps with strong cold calling skills who are highly self-assured, action oriented, and close oriented.

A word about compensation is in order at this point. In sales as in baseball, you get what you pay for. A company that wishes to build a turbo-charged sales team must be prepared to pay its sales reps more that its competitors. That is the only way over the long run

that high performance sales reps can be drawn into a turbo-charged sales force and motivated to keep up the extraordinary level of sales output needed to win consistently in the marketplace.

Once the turbo-charged sales force begins to take shape, it is important to start a mentoring program within it. Experienced sales reps should mentor the mid-level experienced sales reps, and they should mentor the beginner sales reps and trainees. This is a great way to shorten the learning curves of the sales reps and help out those who fall into temporary sales slumps. At one of my clients in the metal fastener business which successfully built a turbo-charged sales force, the Executive Vice President, a remarkable sales champion, supplemented the mentoring program with a monthly "pearls of wisdom" communication from him to all sales personnel. These "pearls of wisdom" covered all elements of the sales cycle, buyer psychology subjects, self-motivation tips, fresh sales presentation humor, new closes, personal development suggestions, and a whole raft of other valuable sales related information. These monthly communications became eagerly awaited and the subject of discussions among the sales reps and between them and their managers. Their educational and motivational impact was significant. Also, regular, formal sales training sessions should be a part of maintaining and improving sales rep skills.

Once the turbo-charged sales force begins to take shape, it is important to start a mentoring program within it. Experienced sales reps should mentor the mid-level experienced sales reps, and they should mentor the beginner sales reps and trainees. This is a great way to shorten the learning curves of the sales reps and help out those who fall into temporary sales slumps. At one of my clients in the metal fastener business which successfully built a turbo-charged sales force, the Executive Vice President, a remarkable sales champion, supplemented the mentoring program with a monthly "pearls of wisdom" communication from him to all sales personnel. These "pearls of wisdom" covered all elements of the sales cycle, buyer psychology subjects, self-motivation tips, fresh sales presentation humor, new closes, personal development suggestions, and a whole raft of other valuable sales related information. These monthly communications became eagerly awaited and the subject of discussions among the sales reps and between them and their managers. Their educational and motivational impact was significant. Also, regular, formal sales training sessions should be a part of maintaining and improving sales rep skills.

The sales reps in every turbo-charged sales force that I have helped to build had an excellent relationship with employees who designed, built, and delivered the product or service that these sales reps sold. These sales reps regularly interacted with these employees at their work stations, occasionally got their hands dirty helping them do something, and often took them out for a meal to show their gratitude for the support they gave to sales.

Finally, building a turbo-charged sales force is not a one time project. It requires constant recruiting and culling. It is a continuing effort.

Over the years, I have seen only a few companies undertake the task of building a turbo-charged sales force, for it involves a great deal of effort, money, focus, risk, and sticktoitiveness. But those firms which tried and succeeded became highly profitable companies where employees, managers, and executives, although working intensely hard, truly enjoyed their work. The winning attitude of everyone in these firms spread into their marketplace and from there to their communities. They became well known and well respected. The original source of this winning attitude was their turbo-charged sales force where winning was what it was all about.

\* \* \* \* \*

Innovation was always a central focus at PSN. Once the company began to secure footholds at some of the major original equipment manufacturing companies, it decided that it needed a vehicle for getting the word out about Pioneer to all companies that purchased industrial fasteners. The Executive Vice President, a true sales and sales management champion, and the company's advertising agency came up with the idea of hiring a professional film production company to shoot a film about PSN at the PSN offices and plant using PSN employees as the film participants. The film which was to be used by the outside salesmen depicted PSN as a fast moving, innovative, highly automated, and the most modernly equipped company in the cold heading industry. This film was shot during working hours and really reflected the pace, excitement, and positive atmosphere of the company. The film was shown by the outside sales reps using a portable projector to purchasing agents, engineers, and decision makers. It was a very expensive investment in the company's sales effort, and it probably had a greater impact internally than it did externally (an example of the Hawthorne Effect.) The espirit de corps, pride in employment, loyalty, and commitment to do anything that was required to satisfy the customer that it generated was tremendous. Other innovative thinking of the company which strengthened it was the openness to the hiring of qualified minorities and women, the promotion of women to management positions, and the keeping of paperwork and meetings to a minimum. It is interesting to note that many of the interoffice memos were handwritten notes on sheets of legal pad paper rather than typed memos produced by secretaries.

Another aspect of this very successful company was the design and layout of its general office. The general office building was 75% glass, offering to everyone inside a clear view of the outside which was the green belt surrounding O'Hare Airport in Chicago. The inside sales department which took up most of the general office consisted of modern metal desks laid out in rows with no partitions or opaque glass walls. Doors were never closed except in the case of private meetings which were not frequent. General office workers could walk over to each other's work areas with great ease. The office environment was extremely open and conducive to quick and easy communications. Further, the most up-to-date office equipment was purchased for use by office and plant personnel. The only wall in the general office which was not glass was covered with attractive art works that the chairman had collected. Interaction between all levels of workers in the organization was extremely high. At any time one could find the president and inside sales reps interacting with plant workers, plant workers talking to inside sales reps in the general office, computer personnel interacting with the shipping employees, and plant department managers interacting with executives in the general office in their offices or in open areas. Every level in the organization had access to every other level in the organization. There was very little pomp and circumstance in the company, and there was a free exchange of ideas throughout the company. There was not always agreement, but there was a lot of interaction. Also, the president made a habit of managing by walking around. He would regularly tour the plant and talk to the plant workers asking them for their thoughts on various production issues. He rarely asked anyone for a written report on anything. Instead, he would walk up to someone and ask him or her: "What up?" On getting an answer, he would delve into the various issues involved with the person. He would then ask others involved in the same area the same question and integrate the responses so as to gather a body of information that could be used to solve problems or at least form plans of attack to address problems. The president's management style was one of the most effective "management by walking around" approaches I have ever seen. This approach gave him a quick snapshot of any area that he was interested in. He could expand on the subject and delve more deeply into it, or he could move on if he felt that the answer he got was consistent with what he wanted to be happening in that area or what he felt was not a situation about which to be concerned given his top level overview of the organization.

Other corporate culture builders that were employed in the company were special lunch time barbeques for the entire company when one department would exceed its production goal. The issuing of baseball tickets on a random drawing basis to office and plant employees also did much to keep morale high. The philosophy of making employees feel like winners was constantly employed. Regular management training programs were held, and a community relations program was put into place which involved company tours and community assistance. The company quickly became known as a very good place to work. The cafeteria was located in the plant, and all in the general office who wished to eat lunch walked through the plant area, rubbed shoulders with the plant workers, and had their lunch in the cafeteria. The members of the executive committee met once a week to go over progress in their respective areas of responsibility and in the company as a whole. These meetings were short, to the point, and run according to a specific agenda. As I mentioned earlier, meetings were considered a necessary evil. Decision making was largely done individually on the basis of a thorough knowledge of what the overall company objective and corporate philosophy was in the given areas involved in the decision. There just was not a lot of "sending things up" through channels for review, side inputs, or higher level OK's. Decisions were made when needed. If they were correct, and they usually were, the executive would go on to the next decision. If they were not correct, they would be fixed. There was not a lot of time devoted to fault finding. That was one of the keys to success of the company. Most everyone operated like highly informed entrepreneurs. If at the end of the year they "made their agreed upon numbers," they stayed. If they didn't, they were asked to leave.

Experimentation was an important aspect of the corporate culture at PSN. This carried through the entire organization. One example of this was the setting up of a fastener-jobbing company called the "Yes Division." The "Yes" in the name of this entity meant its salesmen would say "yes" in virtually all cases to the customer's request for delivery date or a special configuration or special tolerances. The "Yes Division" became known in the industry as the place to go when you couldn't get something done somewhere else, or you needed a special part in a hurry, or you just wanted someone to cooperate with you on a difficult request. The success of this division was publicized throughout the organization to again reinforce and perpetuate the winning attitude in the company. An important driving force in the company was the belief that was regularly reinforced that everyone in the company was a winner working for a winning organization.

The lean structure, swift work pace, and entrepreneurial risk taking at PSN made for above average turnover, significant stress, and a good deal of difference of opinion. Yet, the company environment was so attractive to the entrepreneurial individuals working there that it had no trouble attracting the most able managers in the area. The interesting outcome of the very progressive atmosphere at PSN was that those who succeeded there really enjoyed their work and those who did not left the company in most cases with only good words about the organization. Clearly, the company's culture, policies, procedures, and business strategy were far ahead of their time.

  At this point, I would like to look at some of the specific techniques that were employed to engender trust throughout the company. I and the other company executives identified the various rank and file employee natural leaders. A relationship was developed with these natural leaders by the top management group and the owners of the company. From time to time, these natural leaders made requests for special consideration of top managers and the owners and vice versa. For example, one of these leaders would ask for an advance on his pay to cover an unexpected bill. This would be granted with no red tape involved. This same leader would be asked later to approach a set-up man to try to convince him to agree to his manager's request to work overtime to fulfill a production need generated by a special customer request. This favor-trading practice solidified the trust of everyone in the company. Workers knew they could rely on management, and management knew they could rely on workers in situations of need. This situation enabled the company to achieve stretch goals. Relatives of plant workers were often given jobs. Special loans for family educational purposes were given to employees in need. The entire organization began to be stitched into a unified effort to achieve company goals. Other symbols were established to differentiate the company from ordinary cold-heading companies and other industrial firms in the area and the country. For instance, the short hand designation PSN was used instead of Pioneer Screw & Nut Company to give the company name a modern ring in a very old fashion, conservative industry. Also, the executive committee was referred to as the "Go Team." The designation "Hot" for rush orders was made into a kind of nickname for various stressful situations. A whole raft of slang words and designations were employed to engender team work, defuse conflicts, and in general provide supportive feelings in difficult situations. It took particularly special kinds of people to keep this corporate culture going. In general these people were open to risk, had positive personalities, had the ability to develop good interpersonal relations, were very money-motivated, and were driven by a high achievement motivation. In other words, they were high achievers doing their thing for money, learning new things, and for the opportunity to test their creativity, resourcefulness, and problem solving abilities. There also was a special sense among the executives and managers of learning the entrepreneurial game. This was borne out by the fact that about ten of the top executives, managers, and salesmen became their own successful business owners after leaving PSN.

The recruiting of such individuals was my job with a good deal of input from the Chairman. The following techniques were employed to attract and retain top level talent:

—a top engineering manager candidate was brought in for interviews on a chartered jet.

—company parties were held at the top hotels in the city.

—a company apartment was maintained for special meetings and as a reward for outstanding performance on the job.

—having the company public relations firm get local radio talk show hosts to invite company executives to participate in their radio programs thereby getting a great deal of free publicity.

—inviting local business school professors to tour the company personally and with their classes.

—regular involvement in local college recruiting programs.

—involvement in the outplacement programs of the local major public accounting firms.

—imaginative employment advertising aimed at building an immediately recognizable identity in the sales, management, and plant labor markets.

—directly contacting standout employees at competitors on a selective basis through PSN's consulting and public accounting firms and advertising vendors.

At PSN no obstacles existed for a proposal if it was seen to have the promised payoff. Proposals for improved operations were always flying around the company. PSN seldom stood on tradition. PSN was a fluid, flexible, fun place to work where most everyone enjoyed coming to work in the morning, although at the end of the day, they were perhaps totally exhausted. The success of PSN was primarily due to its sales strategy. The company's aim was to sell more product than the production facilities could produce and to increase sales by at least 30% per year. This objective insured that the production facilities would always be at full capacity and therefore, job security was provided to all production and support workers. This target growth percentage was chosen so that the company would double in size approximately every two and one half years. The slack between total sales and productive capacity was made up by the Yes Division. This subsidiary sold to customers generated by PSN's sales force and to customers generated by its own inside phone sales group. The Yes Division used PSN as well as other cold heading companies to produce the product it sold.

PSN was a turbo-charged selling machine with highly motivated, bright, production and support workers, and a physical plant, general office, and equipment that were state of the art for the times. The sales engine of PSN was motivated by powerful compensation plans focusing primarily on high impact commission systems, incentive trip programs, constant sales training, coaching, and mentoring, and regular contact between the owners, top management, and sales force. Also, the sales force was always kept at a high level of performance by the practice of letting sales reps go who missed quota three quarters in a row. Further, the company's sales effort was supported by regular advertising, sales materials such as the sales film mentioned earlier, and constant recruiting of top sales resources. Finally, candidates for sales rep jobs were screened through the use of sales aptitude tests and background and reference checks.

Other management approaches that PSN employed to make it the fastest growing firm in the cold heading industry were:
—reorganizing in good times and selectively staffing up in bad times (because that is when the above average employees, managers, and executives, are available.)
—hiring the smartest, most personable, and interesting sales reps with the strongest selling aptitude available.

—establishing a corporate culture which fostered quality in everything, a winning attitude in all employees, a strong pride in employment, and satisfaction from the work performed and entrepreneurial knowledge gained from rubbing shoulders with two of the most successful entrepreneurs in the city—the two owners of PSN.

While at PSN, I wrote an article covering all the major elements of a human resources program that an Inclusive Capitalism company would have. Over the years I have used it in management training programs and in connection with establishing union-free work environments following successful counter-union campaigns. This human resources program is found below in Attachment 3.

Attachment 3 — Establishing An Effective Human Resources Program

The establishment of an effective human resources program can result in important benefits to a firm. In the first place and most obviously, such a program allows for the creation of a positive work environment in which employee morale and productivity can be maximized. Also, a good human resources program will enable a firm to attract the best available employees which will give it an advantage over its competitors.

There are eight basic elements in an effective human resources program: (1) survey employee attitudes on a regular basis; (2) show an individualized concern for employee satisfaction; (3) communicate regularly and forthrightly with workers concerning company progress and direction; (4) treat all employees in a fair but firm manner; (5) maintain compensation and fringe benefits at competitive levels; (6) attempt to gain the allegiance of the natural leaders in the work force; (7) keep the work environment as clean, orderly, and up to date as possible; and (8) avoid hiring workers who do not have the qualifications to perform the work they are employed to do.

The building of an effective human resources program begins with the human resources function. If a firm does not have a human resources person, it should hire one, delegate this responsibility to someone already in the organization and have him/her trained in modern human resources techniques, or hire the services of a human resources consulting firm. If a human resources person is already on the scene, his/her effectiveness should be closely reviewed, and "new blood" brought into the function if performance there is found to be inadequate in the light of causes of any "people problems." The next area to scrutinize is line management. If it is found that members of front line management are weak in handling people issues, they should be exposed to intensive management training.

Organization and communications are vital elements in a good human resources program. Human resources should propose policy, and top management should review and approve it. After Human resources codifies and interprets approved policies, line management give life to them through their everyday directions and interactions with employees. Care must be taken that line management does not over time transfer to Human resources through inaction the day-today responsibility for maintain high employee morale and productivity. Human resources and top management can assist and support front line management in human resources matters, but in the last analysis they are the ones who will determine the success of failure of the company's human resources program.

Therefore, early in the development of a human resources program, a front line management training program should be established. It should provide front line managers with the following information:
(1) Responsibilities and benefits of a front line manager.
(2) Leadership skills.
(3) Human relations and communications.
(4) Basic techniques of management, such as manpower planning, job analysis and evaluation, appraising employee performance, training, accident prevention, giving instructions discipline and discharge, and handling employee complaints and problem employees.
(5) Understanding the management cycle — planning, organizing, motivating, and controlling.
(6) Details of the human resources program, wage and salary structure, salary administration plan, wage payment plan, dress code, and work rules.
(7) Decision making and problem solving.
(8) Keys to management success, such as self assessment and development, effectively managing time, innovation, creativity, and building positive relations with superiors.
(9) Company obligations under employment related government regulations.

Effective communications with management and between management and employees is very important in building employee morale and high productivity. Communication on human resource maters must flow up and down the chain of command. Top management should hold regular meetings with line management and get from individuals the problems they are having in the labor sphere and the gripes they are getting from their employees. Front line managers should hold regular meetings with their employees to get soundings concerning worker attitudes. A weekly ten minute safety meeting is an excellent device for securing information on employee thinking. It can be used not only to discuss safety maters, but also to flush out gripes and problems in their infancy stages. Care must be taken, however, to insure that these meetings are not allowed to degenerate into scheduled gripe sessions or not take the place of meetings between individual workers and their managers to air and settle specific complaints. Formal employee attitude surveys should also be used to learn what employees have on their minds and their degree of company loyalty.

A company that wants to maintain a high level of employee morale and motivation should tell its employees that it has the will to settle employee grievances and wants workers to be an important part of the organization. These attitudes should be communicated to all employees via an employee handbook, general announcements, and orientation programs.

Also the company should, on a regular basis, inform its employees as to the progress of the firm and what direction it proposes to take in the future. Employees are most interested in the condition and plans of their company in that they use this information to measure their employment security and opportunity for advancement. The company should give credit to employees employees for business success which they contribute to and enlist their support in solving problems which they have control over.

The first step in setting up an equitable compensation and benefit plan is to review the compensation rates for competitiveness in the market and for internal consistency. This should be followed by the drawing up of job descriptions and the evaluation of positions, the taking of compensation surveys, the setting of new position and classification rates where required, and the establishing of a compensation plan which relates compensation increases to output levels and provides for compensation progressions which employees consider equitable. Compensation schedules need not be made general knowledge, but if an individual employee asks what the wage progression or salary range is for his/her classification, he/she should be told what it is. With respect to wage progressions, this information should include not only wage rates, but also output levels and time in grade requirements that go with moves from one wage level to another. Openness and honesty in this matter are most important in building trust between employees and management.

Subsequent to the establishment of an equitable wage and salary structure and wage and salary administration system,
a long term employee savings plan should be adopted. This might be a pension plan, profit sharing plan, or 401(k) plan. The next order of business is to establish policy on how temporary assignments to higher paying jobs are determined and what rules guide permanent transfers and bumping. The question of on-the-job training and accumulating company service credit (seniority) should also be addressed, and policy statements on these matters should be prepared.

Some additional programs that build employee morale, motivation, and loyalty are the following:

(1) Company newsletter
(2) Employee e-mail announcements
(3) Partial or complete subsidization of cost of work clothes
(4) Reasonable wash-up time
(5) Company sponsored employee discount plan
(6) Employee activity committee to organize dances, dinners, and sports leagues
(7) Service award program
(8) Choosing deserving employees at random for awards, such as free baseball tickets, paid dinners, etc.
(9) Formal management training for workers aspiring to management positions—to held after working hours
(10) Annual company picnic
(11) Program in which employees represent company ay charitable events at Holiday time
(12) Annual open discussion between employees and top management—small group meetings with President and Human Resources Director to human resources subjects and company progress
(13) Company sports program—partial or full subsidizing of cost of golf, bowling, and baseball leagues and uniforms

(14) Scholarship awards to children of employees
(15) Company paid lunches when production group surpass long standing production records
(16) Suggestion system
(17) Display of company products or services
(18) Sending of flowers to employees and members of their immediate families in the case of illness or mourning
(19) Credit union
(20) Open house for families of employees

It might be said that these programs would be extremely costly or that they reflect a "giving away of the store." Not so! It must be remembered that the taking of the initiative with respect to human resources matters is greatly less expensive than "outsider" intervention. Also, many of these programs can be supported by the monies that are made through vending machines, lunchroom operations and employee activity committee events, such as raffles, picnics, etc. Further, these programs are reflective of a full-blown human resources activity. That is something that the company should work toward. Perhaps it would take five or more years to implement totally. Finally, it should be realized that these programs are the foundation of a plan to make human resources a source of competitive advantage which along with other effective management techniques will insure the maximization of profitability and long term growth in the marketplace.

All employees desire satisfaction from their work, and most want the opportunity to rise to the highest level in their company that their abilities will allow. A firm seeking to prevent serious discontent and low productivity from developing among its employees must clearly show a realization of this situation. First, it must insure that its front line managers recognize that every worker is different and employee motivational techniques appropriate to each worker's individual personality. Second, it should direct all front line managers to learn what the job related aspirations of each of their workers are and attempt to develop each employee to the fullest extent of his/her capabilities. Third, the company's appraisal and promotion system should involve reasonable standards, compensation increases which are based on performance, a commitment to promotion from within, and the use, in tandem of ability, performance, and company service in determining advancement.

Human resources matters must be monitored constantly by top management. They are as important as profit and loss considerations where the work force is potentially volatile. If the company has a management by objectives program, human resources objectives should be included in all managers' performance targets. Through information gained from line management and personal contacts, Human Resources management should keep top management up to date with respect to trends in complaints and work force morale.

All human resources policies, procedures, and programs should be reviewed regularly. Human resources should provide top management with status reports on the operation of all human resources related programs on a quarterly basis. New programs should be added when old ones lose their effectiveness. Employees must feel that management is doing all it can to make improvements in the work environment. Then and only then will the work force trust management, accept changes that might be required to increase productivity, and pull with management with respect to company goals. It has been proven that this approach works. Concern for employees by management will build confidence in management by workers.

All employee expect a safe and orderly place in which to work. Also, their pride in their employment is heightened when they are given modern equipment to work with and regular maintenance is used to keep it in good working order. Attention to employees' needs with respect to their work environment and equipment must be present in all good human resources programs.

Front line management and human resources should maintain close contact with the natural leaders in the work force. Involving these individuals on an informal basis in the determination of new company policy and plans can insure that communication channels between rank and file employees and management are kept open and provide management with information on the acceptability of company action before it is taken. Also, management should consider using these individuals as sources for hiring new employees.

Companies should be careful to screen prospective employees properly and train new hires. The hiring of workers who are not qualified for, or trained to do, the work to which they are assigned, can create serious people problems. Unqualified employees can quickly become frustrated employees, and frustrated employees can quickly become troublemakers. Hiring high potential employees must be a primary goals of a company's recruiting activity. In depth interviewing, testing, reference checking, and new employee orientation must be employed in the recruiting process.

The following are some additional approaches that can be employed to keep morale and productivity high:
(1) Give awards to front line managers with the least "people problems" and the highest productivity and safety records.
(2) Establish a formal complaint procedure. Use an "open door" policy or "speak out" program involving the choosing of employees at random from each department every month or so to discuss company policy, plans, and progress and provide management which employee thinking on how employees can do their jobs more effectively.

There are situations wherein employee discontent grows because the company cannot develop the profits to provide competitive compensation, benefits, and working conditions. If it is seen that productivity is the problem, management must establish a continuous improvement program. The majority of employees will accept changes aimed at increasing efficiency, even though it means a decrease in the work force if they see that the end result is an improvement for those workers who remain in the company, and layoffs are handled in an equitable manner.

Keeping employees productive and satisfied with their work is not a difficult matter. The key to success is building an awareness of the problems that create employee discontent and low productivity, establishing a program to counter them, and operating the program as an important part of general business operations.

\* \* \*

## Chapter II — How Inclusive Capitalism Will Solve Many of the Country's Economic Problems

Adopting Inclusive Capitalism as a national policy will go far to solve many of the pressing economic problems the country is currently facing.

Inclusive Capitalism's feature of paying a living wage will directly bolster consumption which provides some 60% of the economy. If workers are paid a living wage, they will have more money. If they have more money, they will spend more money. If they spend more money, the economy will grow faster, and prosperity will be engendered. Inclusive Capitalism calls for an end to employment at will and a return to the social compact that says that when a person gets a job, he/she should keep that job unless discharged for cause, such as negligence, stealing, falsifying records, insubordination, deliberately violating a company rule, moral turpitude, and committing a crime. Implicit in this compact is that employees should be allowed through promotion, transfer, and internal training and development to reach the highest level of their competence. Also, employees should be laid off on a last in first out basis and have recall rights. This discharge for cause feature of inclusive capitalism allows for continuity of employment, a most important economic benefit that enables a worker to accumulate savings to realize the American Dream of purchasing a home, providing for the college education of children, and building an adequate retirement fund. The jettisoning of the social compact and its discharge for cause feature and the substituting for them of the employment-at-will doctrine has largely destroyed continuity of employment within the economy and done away with the above mentioned benefits that issue from it. For some years now the clarion call to workers of the prevalent economic theory of Supply Side/Free Market Economics has been "prepare to have three to five careers—not different jobs or employers—in your working lifetime." The payoff of embracing this call is that a worker will for half of his/her working career be working for trainee or beginner compensation. In this situation there is absolutely no chance to realize the benefits of the American Dream.

Continuity of employment has another often unnoticed benefit to the economy. Experienced workers exposed to a company's operations over an extended time within a framework of stable and secure employment often results in greater innovation, creativity, and productivity. A loyal, experienced employee with pride in his/her employment and a secure job in a positive quality of work life organization has the know how and deep experience to greatly improve operations, and by virtue of this positive situation will offer up ideas and innovations that will in fact do so. Two examples of the important operational value that long service, highly experienced workers provide a company are seen in the case of the Firestone Tire & Rubber Company's use of inexperienced strike replacement workers at one of its tire plants that resulted in alleged poor quality tires that were placed on Ford Explorer SUVs and the case of Boeing moving portions of its assembly operations from its long established Washington plant work force to a new plant work force in South Carolina that resulted in serious manufacturing delays.

    Another aspect of Inclusive Capitalism involves training current employees for jobs up the organizational ladder and hiring and training qualified applicants for entry level job openings.

Training new hires and not going outside the company or outside the country to hire experienced persons, unless it is a must to do so, would do much to alleviate the unemployment problem. Further, a company that has a training program from entry level upward through the organization offers the economy a much more efficient way to impart skills and experience to new arrivals to the work force as well as to those already in it than the governmental and private skills training organizations scattered around the country that often do not offer up to date, state of the art, specifically targeted programs. In-house training provides the exact training needed in the exact place, in the exact measure and structure for the exact amount of time. A case in point here is the PSN in-house Headerman Training Program described in the preceding chapter. Admittedly, in-house skills training is expensive. However, in the next chapter there will be a discussion of the use of tax incentives to offset the costs of in-house skills training.

Paying a living wage when coupled with providing continuity of employment provides an important benefit to the financial health of the country. Steady employment at living wages and above result in more paid Social Security taxes, more paid income taxes, more paid sales taxes and less reliance on the social safety net programs which results in greater tax revenue, less deficit spending, and the increased ability to pay down the national debt and arrive at a national budget that is balanced or in surplus.

Profits sharing is another important aspect of Inclusive Capitalism. Such a program adds to the worker's financial ability to attain the American Dream mentioned above.

Other aspects of Inclusive Capitalism involve quality of work life matters such as open communications up and down the organization with regular employee "speak out meetings", performance appraisal programs that tell employee when they stand and what their future opportunities might be, new employee orientation and company culture meetings, and employee activities like company picnics, bring your family to work days, and holiday parties. These company programs provide workers with pride in employment and job satisfaction and employers with worker loyalty and commitment, all important social values.

So here we have a picture of Inclusive Capitalism reversing

the inequality of income, alleviating the Middle Class Squeeze, helping to return the American Dream, stimulating the economy, taking pressure off the social safety net, decreasing the deficit and national debt, helping to bring the budget into balance or surplus, and providing workers with a quality of work life that will increase productivity, innovation, creativity, job satisfaction, pride in employment, and company loyalty. Clearly, Inclusive Capitalism is a win-win solution all around. But how might this reformation in our economic system be brought about? I see only one approach that has a chance of succeeding. The next chapter will take up this matter.

## Chapter III — The Road to Inclusive Capitalism, A New Set of Labor Laws and a New Business School Curriculum

Much has recently been said about resurrecting the American labor movement and stimulating employee cooperatives as means to bring about some of the effects that issue from Inclusive Capitalism. The Employee Free Choice Act (EFCA) wherein signed union authorization cards could be substituted for NLRB representation elections was talked about to give the union movement and collective bargaining a resurgence. Political support for the EFCA disappeared, and although the number of worker run companies is increasing, the employee cooperative movement has made no significant economic impact on the economy.

America is a country with deep entrepreneurial roots. Inclusive Capitalism will only come about if it is embraced by the American business class. And in my view, the only way it will be embraced by this group is if it offers a financial incentive to do so.

Let us start the discussion of how Inclusive Capitalism might be substituted for the current Supply Side/Free Market economic ideology by looking at the current mainstream Progressive ideological position dealing with labor relations in America, unions, and reestablishing collective bargaining as a means to decrease income inequality, alleviate the Middle Class Squeeze, and return the American Dream.

The discussion starts with globalization. Globalization has made current American labor laws that encourage collective bargaining and allow for adversarial labor-management relations totally obsolete. The lawyer authored, adversarial system upon which current American labor law is based must be replaced by an organization development based labor law system. Should adversarial employer-employee relations spring up in a firm that is or becomes unionized, its viability will certainly be threatened by foreign competition. In our globalized world, there no longer is a place for conflict ridden union drives and counter-union campaigns, protracted collective bargaining negotiations, slowdowns, strikes, boycotts, phony grievances, or extended adjudication of unfair labor practices. In this age of globalization, the entire company must pull together or it will become in danger of quickly being driven out of business by low wage foreign or domestic competitors. As a human resources consultant with significant experience in counter-union campaigns and establishing positive employee relations programs, it is clear to me that firms which become unionized lose their ability to improve or even maintain their edge in the marketplace. Union free firms are the ones that rise to the top of their industry in terms of growth rates, profitability, innovation, and employee satisfaction. There is no substitute for an organization of highly motivated employees with a winning attitude who consistently pull together. Unionized firms, unless they adopt a program of extraordinary employer-union cooperation, will quickly become dinosaurs in their industry and fade away as important players.

  Another aspect of the need to revise America's labor laws has to do with the decline of the middle class. It is true that unions were instrumental in building the middleclass in America. As a result of globalization the middle class is under assault and shrinking. Since unions have no chance of regaining their former place in the American economy due to the rise of globalization, something else must take it place to rebuild the middle class and insure the economic progress and stability which the middle class has provided. The continuity of employment which job security policies provide, the rising take home pay provided by progressive pay programs, and the steadily increasing skill status which seniority and job bidding programs offer and the attendant job satisfaction, company loyalty and work motivation and innovation must be reestablished to give financial stability to the middle class which is so vital to steady economic growth, sufficient national savings, and social stability. Since unionism can no longer provide these things. Something else must. The answer is Inclusive Capitalism supported by a revised set of labor laws built around organization development principles, overseen by the federal government, and energized through tax incentives. Government must provide the countervailing power to corporations and businesses in general which in very many instances have become extraordinarily powerful.

The field of organization development has identified what labor-management relations should look like in a highly successful firm. The basis of the very successful business is a highly motivated employee team which consistently innovates at the level of product or service, managerial system, and customer service.

A new set of labor laws based on the following principles should be enacted and companies should be motivated to adopt them through meaningful tax incentives:
—Employment rights should be determined by the employment-at-will legal doctrine through six months of company service and then based on the social compact of accumulated company service (last in first out) and discharge for cause. (Seniority rights.)
—Informing all employees what their employment requires in terms of performance and what their employment offers in terms of compensation, benefits, etc. For example, this

would cover how the wage payment, salary administration, performance evaluation, and discipline programs work, what the benefits are, what the corporate culture is all about, and how promotions and transfers are handled. Orientation programs and an employee handbook can handle these matters.

—Progressive compensation—an employee's pay rises as he/she reaches and surpasses the fully qualified level of performance. If a job takes twenty-four months to learn and an employee is partially qualified to perform the job, he/she should expect progressive pay increases until he/she reaches the fully qualified level of performance—perhaps a period of nine to twelve to eighteen months.

—Employee monetary bonuses. Just as entrepreneurs and corporate managers and executives are motivated by money so also are rank and file employees. It's what Frederick Herzberg found seventy-five years ago, Nothing has changed here.

—Comprehensive employee training and development

programs to insure upward movement of ability and talent in the organization. These training programs should include apprenticeship programs for both trade jobs and white collar jobs such as programmers, systems designers, and computer technicians and troubleshooters.

—Open communications up and down the organization (regular employee speak-out sessions.)

—Performance appraisal systems that evaluate employee performance regularly.

—Profit sharing for all employees with seniority rights.

—Meaningful tax incentives for firms that adopt organization development based employee relations programs.

Organization development based human resources programs such as these overlain on current workplace laws will provide a powerful economic system characterized by high employee motivation and satisfaction, improved quality of life, and evident workplace fairness. However, if employees are not satisfied with the operation of an organization development human resources program, they could still take the steps required to try to vote in a union under the NLRA.

Further, a change in the content and thrust of business school education is required to get Inclusive Capitalism moving into the American economy. Books such as the instant one should be written by general economists, labor economists, organization development experts, psychologists, political scientists, and public administration specialists and introduced into the curricula of American business schools.

The question regarding this proposal will become: will over the long run, low labor cost, low motivation foreign and domestic competition swamp high motivation, high labor cost, high employee satisfaction, high quality of work life, and high productivity producers? The answer is some will and some won't, depending on the cost structure, nature of the product or service, nature of the technology, and comparative work force motivation levels. Nevertheless, it is better from a societal point of view that the creation/destruction forces in the economy be driven by worker and organization productivity factors along with other organization development factors than by comparative labor cost factors alone.

This proposal transfers the major drivers in labor-management matters from attorneys to human resources professionals. My experience indicates that this will be a positive transformation in that it will transform the labor-management interaction which is prone to conflict with a system involving conflict avoidance and conflict resolution based not on relative power positions but on rational, win-win solutions. Also, it will show the benefits of enlightened employer-employee relations to corporations and entrepreneurs and will re-establish the human resources function as a major player in the organizational hierarchy of American business. Further, this new system of employer-employee relations will support greater continuity of employment which will raise the accumulated skill level of employees, potentially increase their long run net worth, which would have significant societal benefits, and rid the workplace of adversarial attitudes and activities which are so harmful to high morale, productivity, and initiative and innovation.

What are the chances that such a new labor relations legal system will be enacted? Virtually none at this time. Our legislators know next to nothing about the field of organization development. Further, many of our legislators are attorneys who would not like to see a major practice area removed from their area of professional involvement.

Nevertheless, Inclusive Capitalism as seen in this new system of employer-employee relations and business school education is what the economy needs in this era of globalization. It does not matter if it has a strong chance of adoption at this time. Eventually, it will be seen as the correct path to take in labor-management relations.

www.ingramcontent.com/pod-product-compliance
Lightning Source LLC
Chambersburg PA
CBHW071803170526
45167CB00003B/1150